# CHANGING WORLD

# INDIA

## Rob Bowden and Darryl Humble

### FRANKLIN WATTS
LONDON • SYDNEY

First published in 2008 by Franklin Watts

© 2008 Arcturus Publishing Limited

Franklin Watts
338 Euston Road
London NW1 3BH

Franklin Watts Australia
Level 17/207 Kent Street, Sydney, NSW 2000

Produced by Arcturus Publishing Limited,
26/27 Bickels Yard, 151–153 Bermondsey Street, London SE1 3HA

The right of Rob Bowden and Darryl Humble to be identified as the authors of this work has been asserted by them in accordance with the Copyright, Designs and Patents Act 1988.

Series concept: Alex Woolf
Editor and picture researcher: Cath Senker
Designer: Ian Winton
Illustrator: Stefan Chabluk

Picture credits:
Corbis: cover *left* (Jeremy Horner), cover *right* (Jacqueline M Koch), 8 (Diego Lezama Orezzoli), 10 (Stapleton Collection), 12 (Bettmann), 13 (Kapoor Baldev/Sygma), 21 (B Mathur/Reuters), 22 (Jayanta Shaw/Reuters), 25 (Reuters), 37 (Andrew Holbrooke).
EASI-Images (photos by Rob Bowden unless otherwise stated): title page, 9 (Jenny Matthews), 11, 15, 17, 18, 19, 24, 26, 27, 28, 29, 30 (Chris Fairclough), 31, 33, 34 (Chris Fairclough), 38, 39 (Chris Fairclough), 40 (Chris Fairclough), 41 (Amit Gupta/Reuters), 42 (Chris Fairclough), 43 (Chris Fairclough).

The illustrations on pages 7, 14, 16, 20 and 27 are by Stefan Chabluk.

Cover captions:
Left: A nine-year-old Nepali girl harvests tea on Peshok Tea Estate.
Right: A wind farm near Bada Bagh in Rajasthan.

Every attempt has been made to clear copyright. Should there be any inadvertent omission, please apply to the publisher for rectification.

A CIP catalogue record for this book is available from the British Library.

Dewey Decimal Classification Number: 915.4

ISBN 978 0 7496 8207 1

Printed in Malaysia

Franklin Watts is a division of Hachette Children's Books, an Hachette Livre UK company.
www.hachettelivre.co.uk

# Contents

# CHAPTER 1

# A Country of Many

India's 1.1 billion people accounted for 17 per cent of the global total in 2006, second only to China in terms of population. Spread across an area more than 12 times the size of the UK, India has a huge range of landscapes. These include the high mountains of the Himalayas, the arid Thar Desert of Rajasthan, the fertile Gangetic plains and the coastal wetlands of the Sundarbans. India's people vary almost as much as its landscapes, with around 415 ethnic groups and dozens of religions. Society is further diversified by the caste system, a local class system that affects people's education, employment and even relationships.

## Times of change

India has only existed as a modern state since the end of British rule in 1947. Since then, India has undergone enormous social, economic, political and environmental changes. India's population has almost trebled, and by 2006 its economy was one of largest in the world. India also has a growing influence in global trade and politics. However, not all of the changes have been for the good. Around 25 per cent of the population live in poverty, and the gap between India's rich and poor continues to widen. The pace of development has also been costly for the environment. Forests have been cleared for fuel or land, many rivers are little better than open sewers, and in many cities the air is so thick

**GEOGRAPHIC STATISTICS**

Land area: 2,973,190 sq km
Longest river: Ganges 2,510 km
Highest point: Kanchenjunga 8,598 m
Lowest point: Indian Ocean 0 m
Neighbours: Bangladesh, Bhutan, Burma, China, Nepal, and Pakistan

Source: UN Agencies; CIA World Factbook

with fumes from industry and traffic that it is a major health hazard.

## Opportunities

Despite the challenges, India can be optimistic about its future and the opportunities ahead. It has a stable democratic system, one of the world's fastest growing economies, and a well-educated and hard-working population. The 60 years since independence have changed India beyond all recognition, but many experts believe the next 60 will be the most important in the country's long and turbulent history.

*(Opposite)* **This map of India indicates the country's main geographical features and the main places mentioned in this book. The inset map shows where India is in the world.**

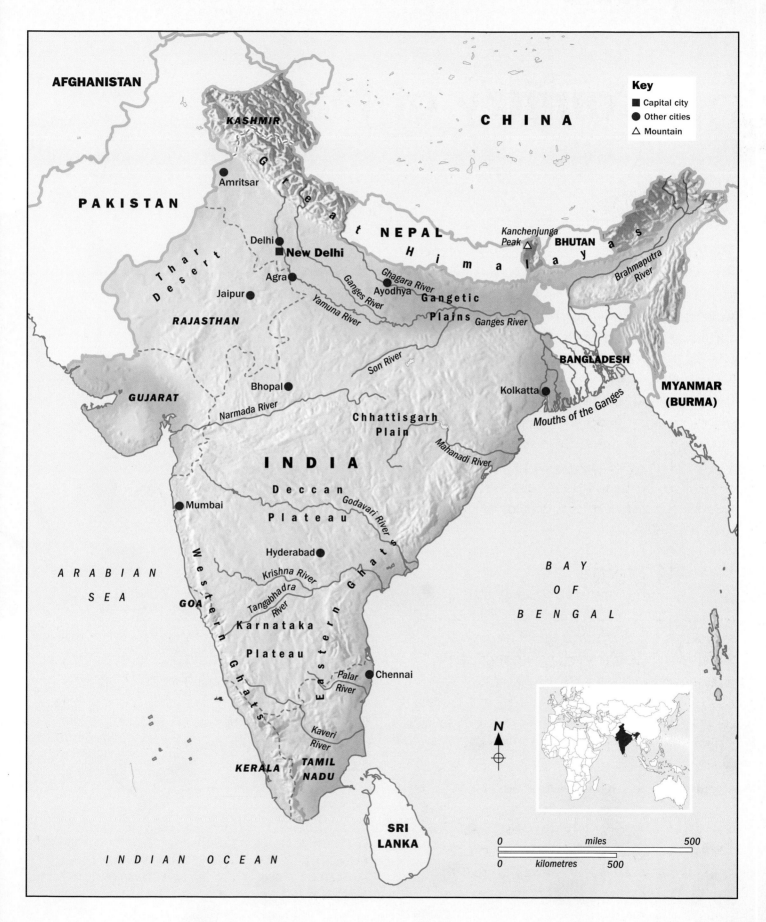

AFGHANISTAN

CHINA

KASHMIR

**Key**
■ Capital city
● Other cities
△ Mountain

PAKISTAN

Amritsar

*G r e a t*

NEPAL

Kanchenjunga
Peak △ BHUTAN

*H i m a l a y a s*

Delhi
■ **New Delhi**

Agra

Ghagara River
Ayodhya

Brahmaputra
River

*T h a r
D e s e r t*

Jaipur

Ganges River

Gangetic
Plains

Ganges River

RAJASTHAN

Yamuna River

Son River

BANGLADESH

MYANMAR
(BURMA)

GUJARAT

Bhopal

Kolkatta

Narmada River

Chhattisgarh
Plain

Mouths of the Ganges

Mahanadi River

**I N D I A**

Deccan

Mumbai

Plateau

Godavari River

ARABIAN

Hyderabad

B A Y

SEA

Krishna River

O F

GOA

*Western Ghats*

Tangabhadra
River

B E N G A L

Karnataka

Plateau

*Eastern Ghats*

Palar
River
Chennai

Kaveri
River

N

KERALA

TAMIL
NADU

SRI
LANKA

INDIAN OCEAN

0          miles          500

0     kilometres     500

# CHAPTER 2

# History

India's long and complex history has involved the continuous movement of people for more than 5,000 years. The earliest evidence of major settlement dates back to the Indus civilization of north-western India (now part of Pakistan), in around 2500 BCE. Archaeologists have shown that the Indus people were highly skilled and survived on farming and trade. Their civilization lasted for over 1,000 years; at its peak, it extended over an area one-third of India's current size.

During the period 1500–200 BCE, Aryan (or Indo-European) people began to arrive and settle in India. Elements of their culture, including languages and religious beliefs, are still found in India today.

The Aryan settlers also introduced new forms of warfare and trade to India. These were to influence the history of India for the following thousand years, helping to shape some of its great empires and uniting vast areas of northern India. The period of empire introduced yet more new ideas. During this period, several new religions were formed in India, including Buddhism and Jainism around the fifth century BCE.

## The Mughal Dynasty

Muslims first began arriving in India around 700 CE, and over the following centuries they made several attempts to gain control of the region. They did not succeed until 1192, when the

**The ruins of Mohenjo-Daro (now in Pakistan) were discovered by archaeologists in the 1920s. The city was an important trading centre and dates back to the Indus Valley civilization (c. 2500–1700 BCE).**

The period of Shah Jahan's rule (1628–58) is one of the best-documented periods of Mughal rule. Shah Jahan was responsible for the architectural masterpiece of the Taj Mahal. Every year it is estimated that between 2 and 3 million visitors visit the Taj Mahal.

Sultanate (kingdom) of Delhi was established, and northern India became united under Muslim rule. The sultanate held power for nearly 200 years; then in 1392 Delhi was overthrown by Mongol armies from the east. Muslim armies regained control in 1526, and India came under a series of rulers known as the Mughals. The Mughal emperors held on to power until 1858, when Bahadur Shah Zafar II was deposed by the British.

## European interest: from trade to empire

In 1498 the Portuguese explorer Vasco da Gama reached India, returning with stories of great riches. The Portuguese established trading posts to take advantage of the spices, silk and other natural wealth that India had to offer and they were closely followed by other European powers of the time. In an effort to seize control of this profitable export trade, the British, Dutch, Portuguese and French began to make claims on Indian territory. In the struggle that followed, the British East India Company emerged as the most powerful force in the region. Between 1600 and 1857 the company, backed by its own military forces, established control across much of India.

### COMPARING COUNTRIES: THE RICHES OF THE COLONIES

Under British rule, India was exploited for its agricultural produce, including spices, sugar, tea, coffee, cotton and indigo. Other British colonies, such as South Africa, were exploited for their mineral deposits, including metals, gold, diamonds and coal.

During the Indian Mutiny, the Siege of Lucknow became a major point of conflict between Indian rebels and the British administration. By the end of the siege, many parts of Lucknow had been destroyed.

By the mid-nineteenth century, the control of the British East India Company over the Indian economy had become extremely unpopular. The Indian people were forced to pay rent on farmland and to replace traditional food crops with ones that could be sold for export. As a result of these measures, they were unable to feed themselves adequately. They began to protest. In 1857 a series of uprisings broke out, which became known as the Indian Mutiny. The British defeated the uprising, but it cost many lives and demonstrated the weakening control of the British East India Company.

India's exports were by now very important to the British economy, and Britain did not want to lose them. To protect its interests, the British government replaced the British East India Company in 1858 and declared India part of the British Empire. Queen Victoria became Empress of India, and a viceroy was appointed to manage India on the behalf of the queen. India was now the responsibility of the British government, and so political as well as economic decisions were made in the British parliament.

## The struggle for independence

British rule remained unpopular, and there was a growing campaign for independence. The campaign became fully established when a young lawyer and political campaigner called Mohandas K. Gandhi returned to India from South Africa in 1915. He formed an alliance with Jawaharlal Nehru. Gandhi and Nehru had both been educated in British universities and together led the movement for a free and independent India. Their movement was noted for its non-violent approach, using tactics of non-cooperation (refusing to obey British rules and laws) to defy British rule. The Salt Marches of 1930 were an important example of such actions.

After World War II (1939–45), Britain was severely weakened and unable to maintain control of its vast empire. The government appointed Lord Louis Mountbatten as viceroy to begin

## BRITISH COLONIES AND DATES FOR INDEPENDENCE

Most British colonies gained their independence during the twentieth century.

| Country | Date of colonization | Date of independence |
|---------|----------------------|----------------------|
| Australia | 1829 | 1901 |
| Egypt | 1914 | 1922 |
| India | 1858 | 1947 |
| Jamaica | 1866 | 1962 |
| Kenya | 1920 | 1963 |

negotiations for India's independence from Britain. The move to independence was far from simple (see page 12) but on 15 August 1947, India finally gained its freedom. Jawaharlal Nehru became India's first prime minister in a government led by the Indian National Congress. One of the government's first actions was to create an Indian constitution, which was completed in 1950. It recognized India as a secular state with the aim to protect the democratic rights of all citizens. This was an ambitious task for a country made up of so many different peoples, and maintaining stability has been a central challenge for all of India's leaders.

**In defiance of a law banning Indians from producing their own salt, Gandhi led a 385-km march across western India to collect salt from Dandi on the coast.**

**Many men were caught up in the violence that followed partition, leaving women and children to flee and begin life as refugees. These women and children are in Amritsar, having fled Pakistan.**

## FOCUS: PARTITIONING INDIA

The promise of independence led to a power struggle between India's many different peoples. The most significant tensions were between Hindus, Muslims and Sikhs, who all wanted their own independent states. As a result, British-controlled India was to be partitioned (divided) into two states. India would be for the Hindus and Pakistan for the Muslims. Sikh leaders failed to secure the Punjab as an independent state and were mostly absorbed into India. The final lines of partition created the mainly Muslim states of East Pakistan (now Pakistan) and West Pakistan (now Bangladesh) to either side of a mainly Hindu India. This led to the world's largest mass migration as more than 12 million Hindus and Muslims moved to their new states. During this process, tension between the different faiths led to violent clashes, and an estimated half a million people were killed. The issue of partition has never been finalized, and relations between India and Pakistan remain tense.

## Indira Gandhi and the Emergency

Following independence India underwent major developments in farming and industry with the introduction of new technologies and ideas. Despite such progress, major social and economic problems remained and were aggravated by a fast-growing population. By the 1970s, poverty, food shortages and a large increase in the price of oil threatened to ruin India's young and fragile economy. With growing social and political unrest, Prime Minister Indira Gandhi (daughter of Nehru), introduced a State of Emergency in 1975. In order to keep control, some basic freedoms were taken away, such as the freedom of speech.

The State of Emergency continued until 1977, when Indira Gandhi lost power in the elections, only to be re-elected in 1980. She caused a crisis in 1984 when she ordered troops to storm the Golden Temple in Amritsar to remove Sikh protesters who had occupied their holy temple to demand that Punjab become an independent Sikh state. Some 300 Sikhs were killed, and the temple was badly damaged. Later that year Indira Gandhi was assassinated (murdered) by two of her Sikh bodyguards in an act of revenge for the storming of the Golden Temple.

## Looking to the world

Following the death of Indira Gandhi, her son Rajiv Gandhi became prime minister until he too was assassinated in 1991. Rajiv Gandhi was the first of several modernizing prime ministers who began to encourage foreign investment in India and promote its skilled workforce. Despite several periods of instability, the country held together politically, and the economy began to grow. As India approached the new millennium, it had become established as a major global economy, among the fastest growing in the world. This growth has continued into the new millennium, increasing the pace of change and providing new opportunities. Nevertheless, with a population of more than one billion, around a quarter of whom still live in poverty, India's challenges are far from over.

**Indira Gandhi was one of India's most successful, but also most controversial Prime Ministers. Members of her family followed her into politics; in this photograph, her son Rajiv is on her right. The Gandhi family remain key political leaders today.**

# CHAPTER 3

# Social Changes

India's greatest social change has been its population growth over the past 60 years (see graph). The annual growth rate reduced from 2.34 per cent in 1966–7 to around 1.38 per cent per year in the early 2000s. Despite this, the total number of people is still increasing rapidly. It is estimated that between 2000 and 2010, the population will expand by about 44,440 people every day! This is because many Indians who were born when population growth rates were higher are only now beginning to have families of their own. They may have fewer children than previous generations, but there are many more people starting families.

The most obvious pressure on a country with a large population is its ability to feed itself. India has made great progress in this area, and food production has more or less kept pace with population growth. Despite this, many people (especially the poorest communities) suffer from food shortages, hunger and malnutrition (a lack

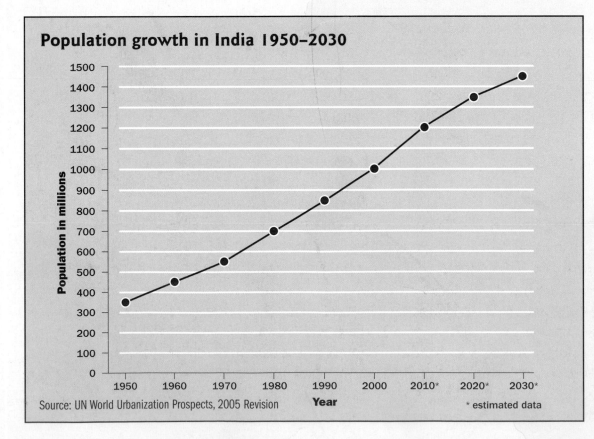

## Population growth in India 1950–2030

Source: UN World Urbanization Prospects, 2005 Revision

*Year*

* estimated data

India's population has grown very rapidly since the 1950s and passed the 1 billion mark in 2000. Growth is now slowing, but India is still expected to become the world's most populous country by 2050.

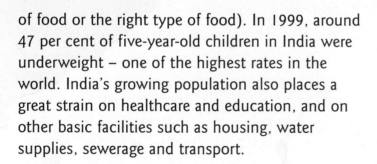

**Informal housing alongside one of the main commuter rail lines in Mumbai. This is typical of India's urban crisis – poor families use any available bit of land to try to set up home in the city.**

of food or the right type of food). In 1999, around 47 per cent of five-year-old children in India were underweight – one of the highest rates in the world. India's growing population also places a great strain on healthcare and education, and on other basic facilities such as housing, water supplies, sewerage and transport.

## A move to the city

India is a rapidly urbanizing society. In 1950, just 17 per cent of the population lived in urban areas, but by 2006 this had increased to 29 per cent. This is partly owing to people leaving rural areas that can no longer support large numbers, but also because the cities have a relatively young population. As these younger people marry and begin families of their own, they add directly to the urban population. By 2030 it is expected that 40 per cent of India's population will live in urban areas.

The effects of rapid urbanization are highly visible throughout India. Cities have become overcrowded, and housing is in huge demand. Many urban residents cannot afford even basic housing and live in informal slum dwellings. These slums are built on unused land in and around major cities and have become major population centres. In Mumbai, an estimated 7.5 million people were living in slums in 2005 – around 60 per cent of Mumbai's official population. In December 2004, the Mumbai authorities began to clear some of the slums as part of a US $6-billion city development plan. The slums were using land needed for new roads and railways or for schools, hospitals and housing. Thousands of slum residents protested against the clearances, and in some areas slum dwellers simply reclaimed the land as soon as the bulldozers had gone.

## IMPROVEMENTS IN HEALTH AND SANITATION

| Indicator | Then | Now |
|---|---|---|
| Life expectancy at birth (years) | 44.3 (1960) | 63.5 (2005) |
| Under 5 mortality rate | 24.2% (1960) | 7.4% (2005) |
| Undernourished population (lacking enough food or the right kind of food) | 39% (1971) | 20% (2004) |
| Children immunized against childhood diseases | 1% (1985) | 58% (2005) |
| Population with access to improved sanitation | 14% (1990) | 33% (2004) |
| Population with access to safe water supplies | 70% (1990) | 86% (2004) |

Source: World Bank 2006–07

## Slow but sure

Despite its growing population, India has made considerable progress in social development since independence. Life expectancy at birth (the average age people live to), for example, increased from 44 in 1960 to 64 years for those born in 2005. This was achieved by considerable investment in healthcare; the number of doctors had trebled since 1960 and the number of hospital beds more than doubled.

Of even greater importance was the introduction of primary healthcare, a programme that combines medical care with preventative healthcare – education to prevent people becoming ill in the first place. In India this has included improvements in the provision of water and sanitation and preventative healthcare such as immunizations (giving injections to protect people from dangerous diseases). In the early 1980s only around 6 per cent of children were immunized against common childhood diseases, but this had risen to almost 60 per cent by 2005.

The results of India's primary healthcare programme are best seen in the figures for the childhood mortality rate (the number of children who die before the age of five). In 1960 this stood at 242 children for every 1,000 live births, but by 2005 it had fallen to 74 per 1,000 and is improving year by year. Nevertheless, childhood mortality in India is still more than double that of other developing economies such as Brazil and China.

## Educating for change

Education has played a key role in improving India's social development, and its education system is known worldwide for producing highly qualified professionals. It has been especially successful in areas such as medicine, engineering and information technology and these skills have played a significant role in India's recent economic growth.

The education system is not without its problems, however. In many areas, schools struggle to meet the high demand from students and suffer from a lack of buildings, teaching materials and even teachers. There is also the challenge of encouraging girls as well as boys to attend school.

This school in Rajasthan provides an education, but a shortage of classrooms means that some classes have to be taught outside. Population growth has placed India's education system under considerable strain.

Traditionally, many girls stayed at home to help with housework before being married and leaving to start their own families. This meant families would often only send boys to be educated. There are still fewer girls in education than boys. In 2005 there were 4 million more girls out of primary school than there were boys. Although this difference is large, the educational opportunities for girls have improved considerably. The proportion of girls completing primary school, for example, increased from 55 per cent in 1991 to 86 per cent in 2005. Another recent change is that girls who complete their primary schooling are more likely to progress to secondary school than boys. In 2005, 85 per cent of girls moved into secondary education, compared to 83 per cent of boys.

## Social inequalities

Gender inequality – the inequality between males and females – is just one of many types of inequality to be found in India. Others include discrimination related to ethnicity, language, religion and caste. Discrimination of any form is against the Indian constitution, but it is deeply ingrained in Indian society and traditionally helped maintain order in the days before a modern political and legal system. One of the challenges for India is that many who benefited from such forms of discrimination in the past, such as people of higher castes, continue to do so today. Because they are already better off, it is easier for them to make the most of India's new opportunities. This means there are still great social inequalities in Indian society.

### COMPARING COUNTRIES: SOCIAL DEVELOPMENT

Although India has made great progress in social development, it is still far behind a developed country such as the UK. Life expectancy for a person born in the UK in 2005 was 79 years, 15 years longer than in India. The number of children dying before their fifth birthday was more than 12 times higher in India than in the UK.

**Western brands such as McDonald's are increasingly popular with India's younger generations and are placing traditional culture under considerable pressure.**

## Modernizing traditions

The caste system is one of the many traditions that can still be seen in India today. Yet with centuries of outside influence, customs that many people consider to be traditionally Indian are often a mix of local and external ideas which Indians have come to call their own. Since the 1980s however, the development of global trading links, improved transportation and modern communications have led to a period of particularly rapid changes. Many younger Indians have fully embraced these changes and seek a modern India with clothing, food, entertainment and pastimes similar to those of the USA or Western Europe. These changes are clearly visible in India's cities and larger towns and are gradually reaching rural areas too.

**Kathakali is a traditional form of story-telling theatre from the south Indian state of Kerala. Traditionally, the performance takes place outdoors and continues for an entire night. The survival of Kathakali is now heavily dependent on tourists, both from overseas and from other parts of India.**

Nevertheless, traditional Indian customs remain alive. Age-old skills, such as the art of block printing used to produce textiles (fabrics), have found new uses in modern fashion and have proven popular both in India and abroad. Other traditions, linked with religion and customs, are also finding new life through the growth of the tourist industry. Both Indians and non-Indians alike are keen to learn more about India's fascinating culture.

# CHAPTER 4

# Political Changes

India is the world's largest democracy. In 2008, 700 million people had the right to vote. It is also a very active democracy – 57.5 per cent of those able to vote did so in the 2004 parliamentary elections. India's political system is extremely complex. In its simplest form, India's political system operates at three levels: national, state and local level (see diagram). The national government has overall responsibility for national issues and is led by the prime minister. State governments have responsibility for local issues, including education, health and transport. In the event of political instability or security threats, the national government can take control of

**This diagram illustrates India's three-tier political system, which has different levels of representation.**

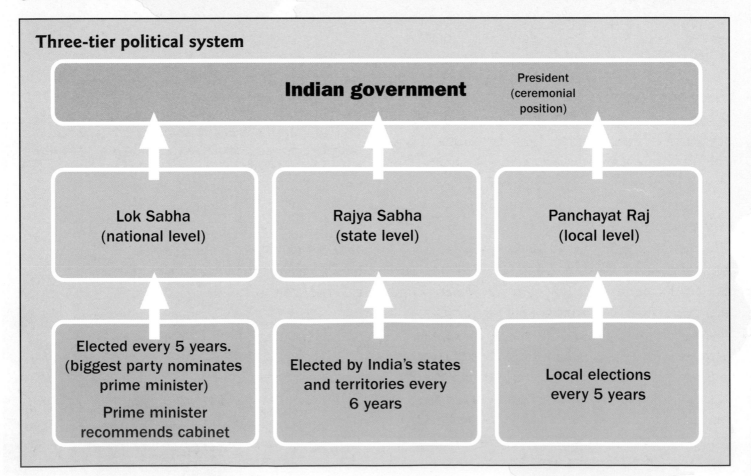

**Three-tier political system**

**Indian government** — President (ceremonial position)

| Lok Sabha (national level) | Rajya Sabha (state level) | Panchayat Raj (local level) |
|---|---|---|
| Elected every 5 years. (biggest party nominates prime minister) Prime minister recommends cabinet | Elected by India's states and territories every 6 years | Local elections every 5 years |

**An Indian policeman keeps guard outside the Indian parliament building. The parliament sits in the Sansad Bhavan – the parliament house that is located in Janpath (meaning 'the People's path'), in the capital city of New Delhi.**

individual states. Local government, known as Panchayat Raj, operates at the district and village level and is responsible for local development and the provision of basic services. It may also be used to deliver state or national policies.

## The three-tier system

The national government has two parliamentary houses, the Lok Sabha and the Rajya Sabha. The Lok Sabha is the main way in which Indian people are represented. Elections are held every five years. The Rajya Sabha (Council of States) is elected every six years by India's 28 states and 7 union territories. Each state or territory has a number of representatives proportional to its population. For example, Tamil Nadu in southern India, with 62.3 million people, elects 18 representatives. Nagaland in the north-east,

with just 1.9 million people, elects only one. Twelve members of the Rajya Sabha are appointed by the president for their expert knowledge in key areas of government.

### COMPARING COUNTRIES: VOTING AGE

Everyone over the age of 18 is entitled to vote in local and national elections in India. This is the same as the voting age in the UK, but older than in Cuba, where it is 16. In Japan, young people cannot vote until they are 20.

The role of president is a ceremonial position with no real political power. The prime minister holds the most political power. He or she is nominated (proposed) by the political party with the most representatives in the Lok Sabha. The cabinet members (the most important government ministers) are then recommended to the president by the prime minister. Elections were last held in May 2004, and Manmohan Singh became India's first Sikh Prime Minister. The most recent presidential elections were in July 2007 and were won by Pratibha Patil.

India's local government system, the Panchayat Raj, is an important layer of government in such a large country. It operates at a district, sub-district (an area within a district) and village level and is formed of locally elected members who serve a five-year term. A key aspect of the Panchayat Raj is that it must include representatives of all sections of society, including women and scheduled castes (see box on page 25).

## Voting in India

Allowing the large and widely dispersed Indian population to vote is a major undertaking. It can take days for votes from remote regions to reach counting centres. The government is continually working to make it easier to vote. In 1989 electronic voting was introduced to provide a faster and

**Before the introduction of electronic voting machines, a high number of votes were not counted owing to mistakes on the voting card at the voting booth. Electronic voting reduces errors and so increases the number of votes actually counted.**

more reliable system. The machines use symbols to clearly represent the different parties. This makes voting easier for the one-third of India's adult population who are unable to read and write.

## Political parties

Political parties in India can be broken down into national, state and independent local parties. There are more than 500 active parties in India, but only 19 managed to secure four or more seats in the Lok Sabha during the 2004 elections. India's major political parties are normally formed around areas of shared interest such as poverty reduction, or have religious links, such as the mainly Hindu Bharatiya Janata Party (BJP).

The Indian National Congress (INC), which was set up during the independence movement, was India's first political party and formed its first government. The party has long been the dominant force in Indian politics. Of the 14 prime ministers to have led India, 8 have been from the INC.

Indian elections never produce a clear winner, so the party with the largest number of seats must form a government by working in partnership with other parties. The current United Progressive Alliance government was formed in 2004 as a coalition of 12 parties led by the Congress Party. Coalition governments allow for a greater representation of India's people, but reaching agreement among the different parties can be a lengthy process.

## Role of women

Women have the right to vote under the 1950 constitution and in theory have equal rights to stand for election. The reality is often very different though. In 2005, fewer than 10 per cent of parliamentary seats were held by women. This is despite a policy that states that one-third of

### CASE STUDY: PEOPLE POWER

Ever since the popular movements for independence, people power has played an important role in Indian politics. There are many examples of people power at both a national and local level, with varying degrees of success.

In recent times people have rallied behind common causes, such as the campaign against the damming of the Narmada River and the flooding of villages to create an enormous hydro-electricity complex. In the Keralan village of Plachimada, local people were successful in 2004 in preventing Coca Cola from over-using local groundwater resources and polluting their environment.

Not all campaigns are successful, however. One example is the lengthy campaign seeking justice for the victims of the 1984 Bhopal disaster. An explosion at a chemical factory in Bhopal released toxic gases that are estimated to have killed between 15,000 and 20,000 people. Campaigners want the factory owners, Union Carbide, to pay compensation (money because of the harm caused) to the families of those who died, but by early 2008, no money had been paid.

government seats should be held by women and the fact that one of India's longest-serving prime ministers, Indira Gandhi (1966–7 and 1980–84), was female.

The Indian government has also tried to promote women's rights at the local level. Since the 1970s it has encouraged the formation of women's self-help groups to help women improve their lives and those of their families and communities. India now has more than two million women's self-help groups, many of which have developed into co-operatives – businesses they own and run themselves.

In Tamil Nadu state for example, self-help groups have purchased land to grow flowers for sale. In other Indian states, self-help groups have become common in the textile and crafts sectors.

**These women are spinning coir made from the dried husks of coconuts. The women work together as part of a small co-operative and sell the spun coir to be made into mats, bags and other products.**

## Scheduled castes

Politics in India continues to be dominated by caste inequality as well as inequality between men and women. Since independence the government has attempted to address the problem. In the Panchayat Raj, one-third of seats are reserved for members of the lower scheduled castes. There have been improvements in the representation of India's scheduled castes, most notably when K. R. Narayanan became the first president to be elected from a scheduled caste in 1997. In 1984 the national Bahaj Samaj Party (BSP) was created to represent scheduled castes and in the 2004 elections won 18 seats in the Lok Sabha.

## Politics and religion

Politics and religion frequently overlap in India, and many political parties are linked to particular religions. As a result, politics and religion can become mixed up, sometimes with terrible consequences. In 1992 there was serious unrest when the Hindu nationalist BJP supported Hindu activists in attacking and destroying a mosque in the city of Ayodhya in northern India.

## FOCUS: CASTE SYSTEM

Indian society was historically structured according to social status with intellectuals and priests at the top and unskilled, illiterate workers at the bottom. Each layer in this system was known as a caste. Traditionally, people could neither move from the caste of their birth nor mix with people from lower castes. The Indian constitution refers to the lowest of these castes as scheduled castes. Although discrimination by caste is outlawed, it still occurs. Strong traditions, not least because they benefit those of higher caste, mean that many aspects of life are still influenced by caste. People from the scheduled castes remain among the poorest members of society. They usually work in the worst conditions, such as in the waste sector or with hazardous chemicals.

They claimed it was built on the grounds of a former Hindu temple, but the destruction provoked an angry response from the Muslim community. An estimated 2,000 people were killed in the violence that erupted. Tensions over Ayodhya re-emerged in 2002 and act as a reminder that Indian politicians have to balance different interests carefully in order to maintain a secular state. A stable political system is vital to India's continued growth as a global economic and political power.

**In 2002, 50 Hindu activists were killed in a fire on a train returning from Ayodhya to Gujarat. A Muslim mob was blamed for the fire and this led to revenge attacks against Muslims in which at least a thousand people (mostly Muslims) died.**

# CHAPTER 5

# Economic Changes

Since 2000, India's economy has grown by around 7.5 per cent per year compared to less than 2 per cent a year in the UK, the USA and in the world as a whole. Many economists believe that India's rapid economic growth will continue to make it one of the world's strongest economies in the twenty-first century. There is support for such claims, but there are challenges ahead too. In 2004–05 for example, it was estimated that 80 per cent of the population were living on less than US $2 per day, evidence that India's economic miracle may not be benefiting everyone.

## Inequality

The caste system has meant that inequality has always been part of Indian society. It has led to huge social and economic divisions that have become more obvious as India has prospered. Official figures on inequality use ratios to see how different segments of the population compare to one another. A common ratio to use is a comparison of average income levels between the wealthiest and poorest 20 per cent of the population.

### COMPARING COUNTRIES: ECONOMIC INDICATORS

India has outperformed growth in the UK economy for many years, but its people remain considerably poorer than those in the UK. The average income for an Indian in 2006 was just US $820 per year compared to US $40,180 for someone living in the UK.

Modern high-rise apartments overlook the Indian Ocean in Mumbai and cast a shadow over the informal slum housing around the shoreline. Stark contrasts such as this are a clear sign of the inequalities found across India.

**Designer boutiques are now commonplace in Indian cities, such as here in Jaipur, but the vast majority of Indians remain too poor to shop in them.**

During the period 1980–94, the wealthiest 20 per cent of society were 5 times richer than the poorest 20 per cent. By 1997 this had risen to 5.7 times richer, showing an increase in inequality. The figures suggested that India's wealthy were benefiting most from economic growth. More recent data for 2004–05 show a slight fall in the gap between rich and poor. This can be explained by a growing number of people moving into India's middle classes (some estimate at a rate of 35 million a year) and by a continuing, but very gradual, decline in poverty.

**This graph shows the rise in India's Gross National Income (GNI). GNI is the total value of a country's economy, including money earned from investments in other countries.**

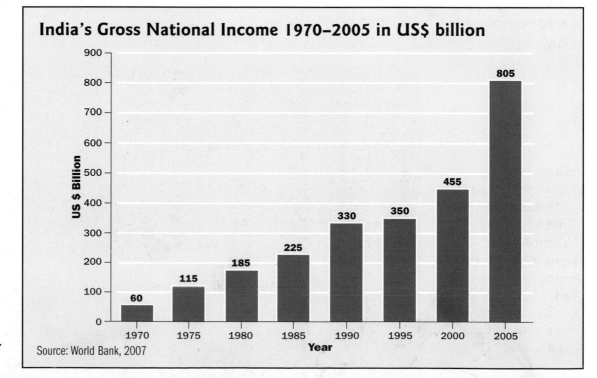

### India's Gross National Income 1970–2005 in US$ billion

Source: World Bank, 2007

| Year | US$ Billion |
|------|-------------|
| 1970 | 60 |
| 1975 | 115 |
| 1980 | 185 |
| 1985 | 225 |
| 1990 | 330 |
| 1995 | 350 |
| 2000 | 455 |
| 2005 | 805 |

Before the Green Revolution, India had fewer than 100,000 tractors or mechanized farm machines, but this figure had increased to more than 2.5 million by 2005.

## Changes in agriculture

India's economy was founded on its agricultural wealth. In terms of employment, India remains an agricultural country, with around 60 per cent of the labour force working in agriculture. In economic terms though, agriculture is less significant than in the past. In 1970 agriculture accounted for almost half of India's national income, but by 2006 its share had fallen to 17.7 per cent. Despite this, agriculture remains vital to meeting India's basic food needs and allowed India to more than double food production between 1970 and 2000.

Much of this achievement was due to the Green Revolution (see focus panel), a change that also led to millions of agricultural workers leaving rural areas to find work in urban-based industries. The Green Revolution influenced far more than India's food production therefore, and can be directly linked to broader social and economic trends such as urbanization and industrialization (establishing industries).

Although India has made impressive gains in food production, they are only slightly ahead of population growth, so the food available per

### FOCUS: GREEN REVOLUTION

The Green Revolution was a package of farming measures, including new seeds, fertilizers and irrigation methods. Introduced to India in the mid-1960s, it was responsible for increasing Indian cereal production from 1,130 kg per hectare in 1970 to around 2,400 kg per hectare today. The impact of the Green Revolution was remarkable for food production and protected India from almost certain famine, but it also brought major changes to the rural economy. Great numbers of India's poorest tenant farmers (farmers who worked on land owned by someone else) could not afford the technology, and many landowners reclaimed land from tenants in order to take advantage for themselves. Millions of farmers became labourers on large farms, whilst others were forced off the land completely because new machinery replaced the need for labour and lowered rural wages.

person has more or less stayed the same. As a result, up to half of Indians continue to suffer from hunger and malnutrition. At the current rates of population growth, India has some 1.3 million new mouths to feed every month! In 2004–05, India was forced to import basic foodstuffs (grains) because it could not grow enough.

The government began to look for ways to further increase food production. In August 2007, it approved trials (tests) of genetically modified (GM) food crops to see if they could help farmers to increase production. Earlier trials with GM cotton in 2001–02 increased cotton harvests by up to 80 per cent compared to non-GM cotton. The government hopes that the GM food crop trials will repeat the success of cotton and help solve India's food shortages. The trials are needed because there are concerns that GM crops could

be harmful to the environment, and possibly to people who eat them too (see Chapter 6).

## Modernizing the economy

Where agriculture has declined in its significance to the economy, modern service sectors such as banking, retail (selling goods), trade, tourism, telecommunications, and research and development have all grown in importance. In 1970 their contribution to national income was 33 per cent, but this had increased to 55 per cent by 2006. A significant factor in this growth has been India's success in attracting European and American companies to outsource some of their work to India.

**New varieties of rice played a vital role in the success of India's Green Revolution and became known as 'miracle rice'. The majority of rice grown in India now is of these new varieties.**

It is estimated that in 2005–06, India accounted for 63 per cent of international outsourcing, which earned India around US $12 billion. Most of the outsourcing work in India comes from English-speaking countries such as the USA, UK, Canada and Australia. This is because of the high level of English spoken by Indian graduates.

The service sector has also grown, owing to a rise in incomes in India. One example is the increase in Internet users from 0.45 million in 1996 to more than 60 million in 2005. The number of mobile phone subscribers grew even faster, from 0.33 million in 1996 to more than 90 million by 2005. Other indicators, such as the number of tourists and passenger air travel, have all doubled over the same period. They show that India has experienced strong growth across the service sector.

## FOCUS: OUTSOURCING

With a good education system and high proportion of English speakers, India has developed a generation of highly skilled workers. The low cost of living in India means that wages are lower than in Western countries. These factors have made India the preferred location for many European and American companies looking to lower costs by moving parts of their businesses overseas. Customer call centres, and data and software management, have been especially successful sectors. Many utility, banking and insurance companies in Europe and the USA now outsource these areas of work to India, where staff costs are around two-thirds lower. In 2005–06 it was estimated that if a US bank shifted the work of 1,000 people from USA to India, it would save about US $18 million in annual costs.

**Growth in demand for Internet services has been extremely rapid in India. This Internet café is in Delhi and similar cafés are now found throughout the country.**

## Women, children and the economy

Women's main economic contribution has traditionally been in agriculture, where they are a vital part of the labour force. The majority of women still work in agriculture, but as India's economy has modernized they have found new roles in manufacturing and the service sector. According to official figures though, the workforce is still male dominated. In 2006 women made up only 28 per cent of the official labour force and just 18 per cent of the non-agricultural

**Women have found many new roles in India's modernizing economy. These women work in a garment factory producing clothes for export to Europe.**

labour force. However, many women work in addition to caring for children and managing the home, but are not counted in official statistics. The same is true for children who work in some areas of the economy such as textiles. Child labour is illegal, but there are always people prepared to risk breaking the law and employ children, who will work for very low wages.

# CHAPTER 6

# Environmental Changes

Industrial development, urbanization and rapid population growth have all placed enormous pressures on India's environment, and there are clear signs that it is not coping. The causes of environmental change can be very different in rural and urban areas, each having their own challenges and responses.

## Rural changes

The Green Revolution has caused some of the biggest changes to rural environments, such as a considerable increase in the area of irrigated cropland. This increased from 18.4 per cent of croplands in 1970 to around 33 per cent in 2003, and has led to water shortages for people and livestock in some drier areas of the country. The loss of vegetation as farming has become more intensive and mechanized (growing large amounts of food on as little land as possible and using machinery) is another problem and has led to increased soil erosion. In response, farmers have increased their use of fertilizers. Between 1970 and 2000, fertilizer use increased almost eight-fold to around 18 million tonnes per year. Yet this has led to problems of contaminated water because rains and irrigation water wash the fertilizer into local water supplies.

A more recent change in rural areas has been the introduction of GM crops. These are said to need fewer chemical inputs and so should be beneficial.

Yet some scientists are concerned that GM crop varieties could contaminate natural varieties and harm the wider environment. They argue that GM crops are a new technology that may have as yet unknown impacts on people and environments.

## Urban changes

India's urban environments have seen a dramatic decline in their general quality. The infrastructure, including roads, rail, water supplies and sewerage, has failed to keep pace with population growth and is under severe pressure. In parts of Mumbai,

### FOCUS: SALINIZATION

Salinization is a process during which soils are damaged by a build-up of salts. The main cause of this is the overuse of irrigation for watering farmland, especially in hot climates with high rates of evaporation. Overwatering leaves excess water on the surface of the soil, which then evaporates and leaves behind the dissolved salts that are found in all fresh water. Over time, the salts poison the soils, reducing fertility or preventing plant growth altogether.

Data from 2005 revealed that some 117,000 sq km of farmland in India were waterlogged (too wet) and therefore at risk from salinization. The same survey showed that at least 100,000 sq km of farmland was already damaged by salinization.

A farmer in Rajasthan checks irrigation pipes used in a drip feed system. This system delivers water directly to the crops and greatly reduces the risk of salinization caused by overwatering.

Kolkatta and other cities for example, existing sewerage systems cannot cope and so raw sewage leaks into nearby rivers and streams. This creates a serious health hazard as well as extremely unpleasant conditions for people living and working nearby. Traffic, especially when much of it comprises older and poorly maintained vehicles, is another problem. Most of India's cities suffer from poor air quality. As a result, breathing-related diseases are a major cause of ill-health.

Cities have begun to respond to the problem. For instance, Mumbai has banned motorized auto-rickshaws from entering the city centre. Their heavily polluting engines were a significant source of air pollution. In New Delhi, the city authorities have begun to address air pollution by investing in the world's largest fleet of compressed natural gas (CNG) vehicles to replace the dirtier diesel vehicles. CNG is a much cleaner fuel than diesel. Several other Indian cities are in the process of converting their public transport to use more CNG.

## Positive signs

There are positive changes in India's environment. Forests, for example, have shown a slight recovery in their coverage over recent years, increasing from 639,000 square kilometres (sq km) in 1990 to 677,000 sq km in 2005. Yet it is less clear how much of this forest remains rich and varied and how much is plantation forestry, such as that used by the tea industry to supply fuel for tea processing. There are signs, however, that natural habitats and wildlife are increasingly valued as a resource in their own right. Eco-tourism, which aims to avoid harming the environment, is one of India's fastest-growing forms of tourism, relying on the country's unspoilt and protected habitats to attract visitors. As incomes have risen and awareness of environmental issues has increased, local interest in visiting India's natural habitats and wildlife is also growing. Visiting one of India's 88 national parks or 490 wildlife sanctuaries (areas where wild animals are protected) has become a popular day out for wealthier Indian families.

*(Opposite)* **Auto-rickshaws offer a cheap form of transport in many Indian cities, but their engines are highly polluting. They have been banned from entering the centre of some cities in an effort to reduce air pollution.**

## Responding to climate change

In August 2002, the Indian government signed the Kyoto Protocol, an international agreement to meet targets for reducing emissions of climate change gases. India will do this through a wide range of initiatives that include planting more forests and converting more vehicles to use cleaner-burning CNG instead of fossil fuels.

Energy production from fossil fuels (oil, coal and gas) is a key source of carbon dioxide, the main climate change gas. In response to this problem, India has become one of the world's leading investors in renewable energy technologies – types of energy that will not run out. These include wind power (India is the world's fifth largest producer of wind power), solar panels and hydro-electricity (power from the sun and water, respectively). Many of these technologies can operate at a local scale and supply energy to remote communities.

Biogas, a gas produced using manure, crops or food waste, is another technology well suited to local energy needs. By 2007, India had some 3.2 million biogas plants in operation, providing fuel for an estimated 33 million biogas stoves.

### COMPARING COUNTRIES: CARBON DIOXIDE EMISSIONS

In 2003 India was responsible for around 4.8 per cent of the world's carbon dioxide ($CO_2$) emissions – the main climate change gas. This is higher than the contributions of more developed countries like Japan, Germany or the UK. However if $CO_2$ per person is considered, India's emissions are much lower at 1.2 tonnes per person per year, compared to around 9.5 tonnes per person per year for Japan, Germany and the UK.

# CHAPTER 7

# Changing Relationships

From early settlers, to invading armies and the arrival of the European colonizers, evidence of foreign influence in India is clearly visible. India has also had considerable influence on other parts of the world. Indian food, for example, is now enjoyed across the world, while Indian designs, dyes and textiles are a key part of the global fashion industry. Since independence, India's role in the international community has changed dramatically. It has become a nuclear state (country with nuclear weapons), developed a highly competitive economy and become a major political power. People now talk of India as a future world leader.

## Indians overseas

Indians have been migrating to other parts of the world for well over a century. Initially, much of this movement was to other colonies in the British Empire and sometimes Indians were forced to move in order to meet the empire's labour needs. Others left India in search of work and greater prosperity, a pattern that increased following independence and continues today. As a result, Indian communities are found in countries all over the world and in some cases have been there for several generations.

Many Indians living overseas have become permanent residents of those countries, but others return to India after a few years. Whether staying short or long term, most Indians abroad keep in close contact with their families in India and send home money, known as remittances. In 2004, the estimated 30 million Indians living overseas made remittance payments worth US $21.7 billion. Besides direct economic benefits, the network of Indians in other countries provides valuable social support and opens up new opportunities for business and trade. Indian companies and the Indian government are starting to recognize the potential of such a widespread global population of Indians.

## CASE STUDY: INDIAN WORKERS IN THE MIDDLE EAST

Since the early 1990s, the south-western state of Kerala has been losing hundreds of thousands of workers (mostly young men) to the Gulf states, where they find work in the region's construction, oil or tourist industries. The families of these workers have benefited from remittance payments, but at the state level there are signs that this mass migration may be less positive. Kerala now has to attract workers from elsewhere in India to meet its own labour needs, and food production has fallen owing to a loss of farm workers. The influx of so-called 'Dubai-dollars' from the Middle East has also caused property prices to rise rapidly in Kerala as workers and their families use their new wealth to purchase land.

**This construction worker in Dubai is one of hundreds of thousands of Indians who have left India to find jobs in the Gulf States. They are attracted by higher wages, which enable them to send money home to support their families in India.**

## CASE STUDY: TATA, AN INDIAN TNC

Indian transnational companies (TNCs), such as the Tata group, are fast becoming global economic powers. Tata has 98 companies that range from food and tourism to engineering and power generation. One of the ways Tata has developed its global brand is by purchasing foreign companies. In January 2007 it purchased Corus Steel (a British company) for US $13 billion to become the fifth largest steel company in the world. In early 2008 Tata Motors was set to take over British car companies Jaguar and Land Rover from their American owners, Ford.

## Global corporations

With around one-sixth of the world's population, India is an enormous market for TNCs. Coca Cola, Nokia and Microsoft are examples of Western-based TNCs that have been successful in establishing themselves in India. Many others are keen to follow their success, but India's growing economic strength means they now face competition from home-based TNCs. India now has its own brands of coffee shops, fashion chains, budget airlines and mobile phone providers.

## Tourists in India

Improved air connections, facilities for visitors and a growing global influence have all made India an increasingly popular tourist destination. In 2005, the number of international tourists visiting India rose to 3.9 million, a 13 per cent increase on the

**A covered rice-boat is punted gently through the beautiful Kerala backwaters in southern India. Kerala is one of India's fastest growing tourist destinations for both international and domestic visitors.**

**The beaches of Goa on India's western coast have long been a popular location for both international and domestic tourists.**

previous year and 48 per cent higher than in 2000. Historically, tourism has focused on a few key locations such as the Taj Mahal at Agra or the beaches of Goa. As transport and facilities improve, new forms of tourism are emerging in India, often linked to particular interests such as religion, wildlife, or arts and culture. Tamil Nadu has developed a tourist industry around its world-famous temples, whereas in neighbouring Kerala, the lush green coconut groves have become the major attraction.

A more unusual form of tourism to emerge is medical tourism. This is when people travel to India to benefit from high-quality medical care at much lower costs than in, say, Europe or the USA. In 2004 more than 150,000 foreigners from around 55 countries travelled to India for medical treatment, and by 2012 it is estimated that medical tourism to India could be worth US $2.3 billion.

## Indian tourists

In 2005 India had an estimated 381.2 million domestic tourists – almost three times the number in 1995. A key factor in the growth of domestic tourism has been the rising incomes among India's middle classes. This new-found

wealth has also allowed more Indians to travel overseas; the number travelling abroad more than doubled from 1995 to reach 7.18 million in 2005. Around two-thirds of these visits were made to countries elsewhere in Asia or the Middle East and many are likely to have been connected with work rather than holidays. Nevertheless, it is clear that Indians are travelling more than ever before.

## International relations

For many years India's relationships with the rest of the world were dominated by post-independence politics and an urgent need for development. Today, India is in a much stronger position and is beginning to lay the foundations for its emergence as a great power to rival the USA and China. India maintains good diplomatic relations with much of the world and is well respected as a peaceful democracy.

### FOCUS: 2010 COMMONWEALTH GAMES

India is a member of the Commonwealth of Nations and in 2003 won the contest to host the 2010 Commonwealth Games in Delhi. The games will be the biggest sporting event held in Delhi and will need major investment in new facilities. The government has committed to supporting the games, but there are doubts as to how much they will benefit the city's 15 million people, many of whom live in extreme poverty on the streets. Some may be worse off as they are forced to abandon their street-based lives to make way for the Games.

India's relations with the USA are especially important. In 2006 the USA accounted for 6 per cent of India's imports, and more than 17 per cent of its exports. With such a high degree of dependence on exports to the USA, any breakdown in relations could seriously harm the Indian economy. The USA is also an important political ally, and has considerable interest in helping India to remain a model of stability in a troubled region. India's status as a nuclear power since 1974 is of particular interest to the USA, especially since Pakistan also became a nuclear state in 1998.

**Sport is hugely popular in India. Cricket is by far the favourite game. Celebrity cricketers are among the wealthiest in Indian society, but cricket is played by people at all levels of society. Even the smallest of empty spaces are frequently turned into makeshift cricket grounds.**

In 2006 the USA agreed to share knowledge around the potential uses of nuclear technology in exchange for India being open about how it intended to use this technology.

## Tensions with neighbours

India's main international tensions have been with its direct neighbours, particularly Pakistan. Most of these tensions are over borders or resources and can in many cases date back to the process of partition. The territory of Kashmir is the most contested issue and has been the cause of several conflicts between Pakistan and India, in 1948, 1965 and 1999. The two countries have also clashed politically over the region's water resources and more recently over the

**The territory of Kashmir is divided between India and Pakistan but both countries claim it. These Indian soldiers patrol a border fence along the disputed area of Jammu and Kashmir state in northern India. They are looking for Pakistani rebels trying to enter the Indian-controlled part of the state.**

development of nuclear weapons. In 1998 India and Pakistan both tested nuclear weapons as a way of threatening each other. The crisis in relations between them was only solved when the international community said it would restrict trade with them unless they stopped the threats. Since then, relations with Pakistan have improved dramatically, and in 2004 the two countries agreed to a peace process to permanently end the conflict.

# CHAPTER 8

# Future Challenges

The changes since gaining independence have brought many benefits to India, including improvements in housing, healthcare, education and employment opportunities. Central to this has been India's political stability. The country has endured some troubles, such as the State of Emergency in 1975 and occasional religious tensions. Nevertheless, its political systems have withstood the pressure, providing grounds for optimism that the world's largest democracy will remain stable.

## Continued growth

India's economic growth has been remarkable, but some economists question whether it can continue. For instance, the success India has enjoyed in attracting outsourcing work is now being challenged by other less economically

**The BKC district on the outskirts of Mumbai is one of the new business and enterprise parks designed to attract foreign investors to come to India.**

**Millions of Indians, such as these people living alongside a major highway, still live in desperate poverty.**

developed countries, including the Philippines, South Africa and China. India will have to further improve the efficiency of the economy, making it easier for international companies and investors to do business in India. Improvements to infrastructure such as airports, ports and railway services are already underway, and major cities are investing in new hi-tech business districts to better meet the needs of global companies.

### FOCUS: INDIA AND BRIC

India, is one of four countries (Brazil, Russia, India and China) that have experienced especially rapid economic changes over recent years. Together they have become known as the BRIC countries. By 2050 the value of the BRIC economies is expected to be greater than the rest of the world put together.

Based on current development patterns, India and China will become global leaders in manufacturing while Brazil and Russia will be the leading suppliers of raw materials and energy. If these predictions prove even partly correct, then India will play an increasingly important role in all of our lives.

## Environmental sustainability

India's air, water, soils, forests, mountains and wildlife have all suffered from a combination of urbanization, industrial development, land clearances and the intensification of agriculture. Rapid population growth has increased all of these pressures, and many natural habitats are now at breaking point. India has recognized that development cannot continue without concern for the environment, and new policies are increasingly being developed to protect it, such as investment in renewable energy and cleaner urban transport policies.

## Sharing the benefits

India's most fundamental challenge is to ensure all Indians share in the benefits of past and future development. It also influences many of its other core challenges, such as protection of the environment. There are signs that equality has improved in India in recent years, but India remains a country where up to 80 per cent of its people live on less than US $2 per day. For these 890 million people, change cannot come soon enough.

**43**

# Timeline

**c. 2500–1500 BCE** Indus Empire develops in the Indus Valley region of north-western India

**c. 1500–200 BCE** Aryan settlers establish a rich trading empire

**c. 321–185 BCE** Mauryan Empire established

**c. 320–500 CE** Guptan Empire established

**1192** Sultanate of Delhi established

**1392** Sultanate of Delhi overthrown by Mongol armies from the East

**1498** Vasco da Gama arrives in India

**1526** Muslim armies invade Delhi and establish the Mughal Empire

**1600** British East India Company is formed

**1857** Indian Mutiny: uprisings against British rule

**1858** Britain defeats the last Mughal emperor

**1858** India becomes part of the British Empire

**1885** Indian National Congress is formed

**1915** Gandhi returns to India from South Africa

**1930** Salt March to Dandi

**1939–45** India involved in World War II as part of the British Empire

**1947** Independence declared; partition with Pakistan

**1948** Mahatma Gandhi killed by a Hindu extremist

**1950** Completion of the Indian constitution

**1971** War with Pakistan leads to Bangladesh becoming an independent country

**1974** India first tests a nuclear weapon

**1975–77** State of Emergency

**1984** Sikh siege of the Golden Temple in Amritsar

**1984** Indira Gandhi is assassinated

**1984** Explosion at the Union Carbide plant in Bhopal kills 15,000–20,000 people

**1987** Troops sent into Sri Lanka on a peacekeeping mission

**1991** Rajiv Gandhi is assassinated during elections

**1992** Destruction of Ayodhya Mosque and religious violence

**1998** Pakistan tests nuclear weapons, leading to a crisis in relations with India

**1999** Brief war with militant groups based in Pakistan

**2002** Further tensions in Ayodhya following train bombings

**2003** India announced as host for the 2010 Commonwealth Games

**2003** Ceasefire declared between India and Pakistan

**2004** India begins withdrawing troops from Kashmir

**2004** Thousands killed as a tsunami hits Tamil Nadu, Kerala and the islands of Andaman and Nicobar

**2007** 68 passengers killed as bombs explode on a train travelling from India to Pakistan

**2007** India and Pakistan sign a new agreement to reduce the risk of future war

# Glossary

**biogas** A gas produced when organic matter, such as manure, crops or food waste, rots to release methane (a type of gas). It can be used for cooking or heating.

**block printing** A traditional method of printing fabric using wooden blocks with patterns carved in them.

**caste** An Indian system in which society is divided into different levels according to traditional jobs.

**civil disobedience** Disobeying laws, normally in protest against their unfairness.

**coalition** A union of different political parties that come together to rule.

**colony** A country or territory governed by another country. India was a British colony.

**constitution** An agreement that sets out the rights of people living in a country.

**contaminate** Polluted by something that should not be there. For example, a river can be contaminated by oil.

**discrimination** Treating people unfairly because of their differences, such as in language, religion or caste.

**empire** The area over which a country has political or economic control.

**ethnic group** A group of people who share a culture, tradition, way of life and sometimes language.

**fertilizer** A product that is added to the soil or water to help plants to grow.

**genetically modified crops** Crops that have been altered by scientists to improve their growth or make them better able to resist disease.

**habitat** A living space that can be as small as a pond or as large as a forest.

**infrastructure** Transport, power and communications.

**irrigation** To supply water to an area of land through pipes or channels to help crops to grow.

**middle classes** The section of society that is neither very rich nor very poor.

**migration** The movement of people, either within their own country or to another country.

**non-cooperation** Refusing to work with someone or with a government, often because you do not agree with what they are trying to do.

**outsource** To conduct part of a business in another place or country because it is cheaper there.

**people power** The ability for a group of people to work together to make things change rather than struggling on their own.

**salinization** A process through which soils become damaged by a build-up of salts, which means plants cannot grow properly.

**sanitation** The provision of hygienic and safe toilet and washing facilities. Proper sanitation facilities can greatly reduce the spread of diseases.

**scheduled castes** The lowest level of the Indian caste system, made up of the poorest people. They tend to do the most unpleasant or most dangerous jobs.

**secular state** A state that is not run according to the rules of a particular religion.

**self-help group** A group of people that work together to reach a shared goal or produce a product or service together.

**service sector** The part of the economy that provides services such as banking, insurance and travel as well as education and healthcare.

**sewerage** The waste from homes and businesses that is carried away in liquid form, from toilets for example.

**slum** A very poor area of a city, where homes are usually built by the people who live there. Slums often do not have sanitation or electricity and water supplies.

**soil erosion** A process in which soils are washed away (by the rain) or blown away (by the wind), making it hard to grow crops.

**transnational corporation (TNC)** A company that has factories, shops or offices in more than one country, but has its headquarters in one location.

**urbanization** A process in which more and more people move from the countryside to live in cities.

**vegetation** The plants that are naturally found in a particular place.

# Further information

## Books

*Countries of the World: India* by Michael Allaby (Evans Brothers, 2005)

*Countries of the World: India* by A. Kamala Dalal (National Geographic Society, 2007)

*Culture in India* by Melanie Guile (Heinemann Library, 2005)

*Global Cities: Mumbai* by Jen Green (Evans Brothers, 2007)

*Troubled World: Conflict – India and Pakistan* by David Downing (Heinemann Library, 2004)

*World In Focus: India* by Ali Brownlie Bojang and Nicola Barber (Hodder Wayland, 2006)

## Websites

http://india.gov.in/
The national web portal for India with links to all government websites and a useful 'Know India' section.

http://news.bbc.co.uk/1/hi/world/south_asia/country_profiles/1154019.stm
The BBC India page with country profile and links to relevant news stories.

http://www.incredibleindia.org/
The official Indian tourism website with a useful 'Know India' section with background information.

http://www.wateraid.org/international/what_we_o/where_we_work/india/default.asp
This WaterAid site provides a profile of India with information about the charity's work to help India meet its needs for clean water supplies.

# Index